# VIOLIN

# 101 BROADWAY SONGS

## Available for
FLUTE, CLARINET, ALTO SAX, TENOR SAX, TRUMPET,
HORN, TROMBONE, VIOLIN, VIOLA, CELLO

ISBN 978-1-4950-5253-8

## HAL•LEONARD®
## CORPORATION

7777 W. BLUEMOUND RD. P.O. BOX 13819 MILWAUKEE, WI 53213

Visit Hal Leonard Online at
**www.halleonard.com**

# CONTENTS

# ALL I ASK OF YOU

from THE PHANTOM OF THE OPERA

VIOLIN

Music by ANDREW LLOYD WEBBER
Lyrics by CHARLES HART
Additional Lyrics by RICHARD STILGOE

Moderately slow

# ANY DREAM WILL DO

from JOSEPH AND THE AMAZING TECHNICOLOR® DREAMCOAT

Violin

Music by ANDREW LLOYD WEBBER
Lyrics by TIM RICE

# ANYTHING YOU CAN DO

from the Stage Production ANNIE GET YOUR GUN

VIOLIN

Words and Music by
IRVING BERLIN

# AS IF WE NEVER SAID GOODBYE

from SUNSET BOULEVARD

VIOLIN

Music by ANDREW LLOYD WEBBER
Lyrics by DON BLACK and CHRISTOPHER HAMPTON,
with contributions by AMY POWERS

# AS LONG AS HE NEEDS ME

from the Broadway Musical OLIVER!

Violin

Words and Music by
LIONEL BART

# BALI HA'I
from SOUTH PACIFIC

VIOLIN

Lyrics by OSCAR HAMMERSTEIN II
Music by RICHARD RODGERS

# BAUBLES, BANGLES AND BEADS

from KISMET

VIOLIN

Words and Music by ROBERT WRIGHT
and GEORGE FORREST
(Music Based on Themes of A. BORODIN)

**Moderately**

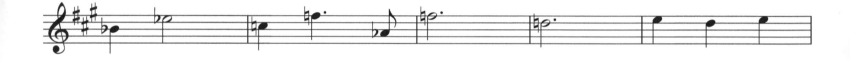

# BROTHERHOOD OF MAN

from HOW TO SUCCEED IN BUSINESS WITHOUT REALLY TRYING

Violin

By FRANK LOESSER

# CABARET

from the Musical CABARET

VIOLIN

Words by FRED EBB
Music by JOHN KANDER

# CAN'T TAKE MY EYES OFF OF YOU

featured in JERSEY BOYS

VIOLIN

Words and Music by BOB CREWE
and BOB GAUDIO

# CIRCLE OF LIFE

Disney Presents THE LION KING: THE BROADWAY MUSICAL

VIOLIN

Music by ELTON JOHN
Lyrics by TIM RICE

**Moderately, with an African beat**

# CLIMB EV'RY MOUNTAIN

from THE SOUND OF MUSIC

VIOLIN

Lyrics by OSCAR HAMMERSTEIN II
Music by RICHARD RODGERS

# CLOSE EVERY DOOR

from JOSEPH AND THE AMAZING TECHNICOLOR® DREAMCOAT

Violin

Music by ANDREW LLOYD WEBBER
Lyrics by TIM RICE

Moderately, expressively

# DANCING QUEEN

from MAMMA MIA!

VIOLIN

Words and Music by BENNY ANDERSSON,
BJÖRN ULVAEUS and STIG ANDERSON

# DEFYING GRAVITY
from the Broadway Musical WICKED

VIOLIN

Music and Lyrics by
STEPHEN SCHWARTZ

# DO-RE-MI

from THE SOUND OF MUSIC

Violin

Lyrics by OSCAR HAMMERSTEIN II
Music by RICHARD RODGERS

Lively

# DO YOU HEAR THE PEOPLE SING?

from LES MISÉRABLES

Violin

Music by CLAUDE-MICHEL SCHÖNBERG
Lyrics by ALAIN BOUBLIL, JEAN-MARC NATEL
and HERBERT KRETZMER

# DON'T CRY FOR ME ARGENTINA
from EVITA

Violin

Words by TIM RICE
Music by ANDREW LLOYD WEBBER

# EASTER PARADE

from AS THOUSANDS CHEER

VIOLIN

Words and Music by
IRVING BERLIN

Moderately

# EDELWEISS
### from THE SOUND OF MUSIC

Violin

Lyrics by OSCAR HAMMERSTEIN II
Music by RICHARD RODGERS

**Slowly, with expression**

# EVERYTHING'S ALRIGHT

from JESUS CHRIST SUPERSTAR

VIOLIN

Words by TIM RICE
Music by ANDREW LLOYD WEBBER

# A FOGGY DAY (IN LONDON TOWN)

from A DAMSEL IN DISTRESS

VIOLIN

Music and Lyrics by GEORGE GERSHWIN
and IRA GERSHWIN

# GETTING TO KNOW YOU

from THE KING AND I

VIOLIN

Lyrics by OSCAR HAMMERSTEIN II
Music by RICHARD RODGERS

# FRIEND LIKE ME
## (Stageplay Version)
from the Walt Disney Stageplay ALADDIN

Violin

Music by ALAN MENKEN
Lyrics by HOWARD ASHMAN
and STEPHEN SCHWARTZ

# GUYS AND DOLLS

from GUYS AND DOLLS

Violin

By FRANK LOESSER

# HELLO, DOLLY!

from HELLO, DOLLY!

VIOLIN

Music and Lyric by
JERRY HERMAN

# HOME

from Walt Disney's BEAUTY AND THE BEAST: THE BROADWAY MUSICAL

Violin

Music by ALAN MENKEN
Lyrics by TIM RICE

# HOW ARE THINGS IN GLOCCA MORRA
from FINIAN'S RAINBOW

Violin

Words by E.Y. "YIP" HARBURG
Music by BURTON LANE

# I BELIEVE IN YOU
from HOW TO SUCCEED IN BUSINESS WITHOUT REALLY TRYING

Violin

By FRANK LOESSER

# I DON'T KNOW HOW TO LOVE HIM

from JESUS CHRIST SUPERSTAR

Violin

Words by TIM RICE
Music by ANDREW LLOYD WEBBER

# I DREAMED A DREAM

from LES MISÉRABLES

Violin

Music by CLAUDE-MICHEL SCHÖNBERG
Lyrics by ALAIN BOUBLIL, JEAN-MARC NATEL
and HERBERT KRETZMER

**Moderately slow**

# I GOT PLENTY O' NUTTIN'

from PORGY AND BESS®

Music and Lyrics by GEORGE GERSHWIN,
DuBOSE and DORTHY HEYWARD
and IRA GERSHWIN

Violin

# I WHISTLE A HAPPY TUNE

from THE KING AND I

VIOLIN

Lyrics by OSCAR HAMMERSTEIN II
Music by RICHARD RODGERS

# I'VE NEVER BEEN IN LOVE BEFORE

from GUYS AND DOLLS

Violin

By FRANK LOESSER

# IF I LOVED YOU

from CAROUSEL

Violin

Lyrics by OSCAR HAMMERSTEIN II
Music by RICHARD RODGERS

# IF I WERE A BELL

from GUYS AND DOLLS

Violin

By FRANK LOESSER

# IF I WERE A RICH MAN

from the Musical FIDDLER ON THE ROOF

Violin

Words by SHELDON HARNICK
Music by JERRY BOCK

# THE IMPOSSIBLE DREAM
## (The Quest)
from MAN OF LA MANCHA

Violin

Lyric by JOE DARION
Music by MITCH LEIGH

# IT AIN'T NECESSARILY SO

from PORGY AND BESS®

Violin

Music and Lyrics by GEORGE GERSHWIN,
DuBOSE and DOROTHY HEYWARD
and IRA GERSHWIN

# THE LADY IS A TRAMP
from BABES IN ARMS

VIOLIN

Words by LORENZ HART
Music by RICHARD RODGERS

# THE LAST NIGHT OF THE WORLD

from MISS SAIGON

VIOLIN

Music by CLAUDE-MICHEL SCHÖNBERG
Lyrics by RICHARD MALTBY JR. and ALAIN BOUBLIL
Adapted from original French Lyrics by ALAIN BOUBLIL

# LET'S CALL THE WHOLE THING OFF

from SHALL WE DANCE

VIOLIN

Music and Lyrics by GEORGE GERSHWIN
and IRA GERSHWIN

# LOVE IS HERE TO STAY
from GOLDWYN FOLLIES

VIOLIN

Music and Lyrics by GEORGE GERSHWIN
and IRA GERSHWIN

# LOVE ME OR LEAVE ME

from WHOOPEE!

Violin

Lyrics by GUS KAHN
Music by WALTER DONALDSON

# LOVE WALKED IN

from GOLDWYN FOLLIES

Violin

Music and Lyrics by GEORGE GERSHWIN
and IRA GERSHWIN

# LUCK BE A LADY

### from GUYS AND DOLLS

Violin

By FRANK LOESSER

# MAKIN' WHOOPEE!

from WHOOPEE!

Violin

Lyrics by GUS KAHN
Music by WALTER DONALDSON

# MAME

from MAME

Violin

Music and Lyric by
JERRY HERMAN

# MAMMA MIA

from MAMMA MIA!

Violin

Words and Music by BENNY ANDERSSON,
BJÖRN ULVAEUS and STIG ANDERSON

# MATCHMAKER

from the Musical FIDDLER ON THE ROOF

VIOLIN

Words by SHELDON HARNICK
Music by JERRY BOCK

# MAYBE

from the Musical Production ANNIE

Violin

Lyric by MARTIN CHARNIN
Music by CHARLES STROUSE

# MEMORY
from CATS

VIOLIN

Music by ANDREW LLOYD WEBBER
Text by TREVOR NUNN after T.S. ELIOT

# THE MUSIC OF THE NIGHT

from THE PHANTOM OF THE OPERA

Violin

Music by ANDREW LLOYD WEBBER
Lyrics by CHARLES HART
Additional Lyrics by RICHARD STILGOE

**Moderately slow**

# MY FAVORITE THINGS

from THE SOUND OF MUSIC

VIOLIN

Lyrics by OSCAR HAMMERSTEIN II
Music by RICHARD RODGERS

# NICE WORK IF YOU CAN GET IT

from A DAMSEL IN DISTRESS

Violin

Music and Lyrics by GEORGE GERSHWIN
and IRA GERSWIN

# OH, WHAT A BEAUTIFUL MORNIN'
### from OKLAHOMA!

VIOLIN

Lyrics by OSCAR HAMMERSTEIN II
Music by RICHARD RODGERS

# OKLAHOMA
from OKLAHOMA!

VIOLIN

Lyrics by OSCAR HAMMERSTEIN II
Music by RICHARD RODGERS

# OL' MAN RIVER
from SHOW BOAT

Violin

Lyrics by OSCAR HAMMERSTEIN II
Music by JEROME KERN

# OLD DEVIL MOON
from FINIAN'S RAINBOW

Violin

Words by E.Y. "YIP" HARBURG
Music by BURTON LANE

# ON MY OWN

from LES MISÉRABLES

VIOLIN

Music by CLAUDE-MICHEL SCHÖNBERG
Lyrics by ALAIN BOUBLIL, JEAN-MARC NATEL,
HERBERT KRETZMER, JOHN CAIRD
and TREVOR NUNN

**Moderately slow**

# ONCE IN A LIFETIME

from the Musical Production STOP THE WORLD—I WANT TO GET OFF

Violin

Words and Music by LESLIE BRICUSSE
and ANTHONY NEWLEY

# ONCE IN LOVE WITH AMY

from WHERE'S CHARLEY?

Violin

By FRANK LOESSER

# ONE
## from A CHORUS LINE

VIOLIN

Music by MARVIN HAMLISCH
Lyric by EDWARD KLEBAN

# PEOPLE WILL SAY WE'RE IN LOVE

from OKLAHOMA!

Violin

Lyrics by OSCAR HAMMERSTEIN II
Music by RICHARD RODGERS

# THE PHANTOM OF THE OPERA

from THE PHANTOM OF THE OPERA

Violin

Music by ANDREW LLOYD WEBBER
Lyrics by CHARLES HART
Additional Lyrics by RICHARD STILGOE
and MIKE BATT

# POPULAR

from the Broadway Musical WICKED

VIOLIN

Music and Lyrics by
STEPHEN SCHWARTZ

# SEASONS OF LOVE

from RENT

VIOLIN

Words and Music by
JONATHAN LARSON

# SEND IN THE CLOWNS
from the Musical A LITTLE NIGHT MUSIC

Violin

Words and Music by
STEPHEN SONDHEIM

# SEVENTY SIX TROMBONES

from Meredith Willson's THE MUSIC MAN

Violin

By MEREDITH WILLSON

# SHALL WE DANCE?

from THE KING AND I

Violin

Lyrics by OSCAR HAMMERSTEIN II
Music by RICHARD RODGERS

# SHE LOVES ME

from SHE LOVES ME

Violin

Words by SHELDON HARNICK
Music by JERRY BOCK

Moderately bright

# SHERRY
featured in JERSEY BOYS

VIOLIN

Words and Music by
BOB GAUDIO

# SOME ENCHANTED EVENING

from SOUTH PACIFIC

Violin

Lyrics by OSCAR HAMMERSTEIN II
Music by RICHARD RODGERS

# SUMMERTIME
from PORGY AND BESS®

Violin

Music and Lyrics by GEORGE GERSHWIN,
DuBOSE and DOROTHY HEYWARD
and IRA GERSHWIN

# SUNRISE, SUNSET

from the Musical FIDDLER ON THE ROOF

Violin

Words by SHELDON HARNICK
Music by JERRY BOCK

# SUPERSTAR
from JESUS CHRIST SUPERSTAR

VIOLIN

Words by TIM RICE
Music by ANDREW LLOYD WEBBER

# THE SURREY WITH THE FRINGE ON TOP

from OKLAHOMA!

VIOLIN

Lyrics by OSCAR HAMMERSTEIN II
Music by RICHARD RODGERS

**Lively**

# THE SWEETEST SOUNDS

from NO STRINGS

VIOLIN

Lyrics and Music by
RICHARD RODGERS

**Moderately**

# THERE'S NO BUSINESS LIKE SHOW BUSINESS

from the Stage Production ANNIE GET YOUR GUN

VIOLIN

Words and Music by
IRVING BERLIN

# THEY ALL LAUGHED

from SHALL WE DANCE

VIOLIN

Music and Lyrics by GEORGE GERSHWIN
and IRA GERSHWIN

# THEY CAN'T TAKE THAT AWAY FROM ME

from SHALL WE DANCE

Violin

Music and Lyrics by GEORGE GERSHWIN
and IRA GERSHWIN

# THINK OF ME
from THE PHANTOM OF THE OPERA

VIOLIN

Music by ANDREW LLOYD WEBBER
Lyrics by CHARLES HART
Additional Lyrics by RICHARD STILGOE

# THIS IS THE MOMENT

from JEKYLL & HYDE

Violin

Words and Music by LESLIE BRICUSSE
and FRANK WILDHORN

**Slowly**

# THIS NEARLY WAS MINE
from SOUTH PACIFIC

VIOLIN

Lyrics by OSCAR HAMMERSTEIN II
Music by RICHARD RODGERS

# TILL THERE WAS YOU

from Meredith Willson's THE MUSIC MAN

VIOLIN

By MEREDITH WILLSON

# TOMORROW

from the Musical Production ANNIE

VIOLIN

Lyric by MARTIN CHARNIN
Music by CHARLES STROUSE

# WALK LIKE A MAN

featured in JERSEY BOYS

Violin

Words and Music by BOB CREWE
and BOB GAUDIO

# UNUSUAL WAY

from NINE

VIOLIN

Music and Lyrics by
MAURY YESTON

**Moderately slow**

# WHAT I DID FOR LOVE

from A CHORUS LINE

VIOLIN

Music by MARVIN HAMLISCH
Lyric by EDWARD KLEBAN

# WHAT KIND OF FOOL AM I?

from the Musical Production STOP THE WORLD—I WANT TO GET OFF

Violin

Words and Music by LESLIE BRICUSSE
and ANTHONY NEWLEY

# WHERE IS LOVE?

from the Broadway Musical OLIVER!

Violin

Words and Music by
LIONEL BART

# WHO CAN I TURN TO
## (When Nobody Needs Me)
### from THE ROAR OF THE GREASEPAINT—THE SMELL OF THE CROWD

Words and Music by LESLIE BRICUSSE
and ANTHONY NEWLEY

Violin

# A WHOLE NEW WORLD

from the Walt Disney Stageplay ALADDIN

Violin

Music by ALAN MENKEN
Lyrics by TIM RICE

# WILL YOU LOVE ME TOMORROW
## (Will You Still Love Me Tomorrow)
from BEAUTIFUL

Words and Music by GERRY GOFFIN
and CAROLE KING

Violin

# WITH ONE LOOK

from SUNSET BOULEVARD

VIOLIN

Music by ANDREW LLOYD WEBBER
Lyrics by DON BLACK and CHRISTOPHER HAMPTON,
with contributions by AMY POWERS

# WRITTEN IN THE STARS

from Elton John and Tim Rice's AIDA

Violin

Music by ELTON JOHN
Lyrics by TIM RICE

# YOU RULE MY WORLD

from THE FULL MONTY

VIOLIN

Words and Music by
DAVID YAZBEK

**Slowly**

# YOU'LL NEVER WALK ALONE

from CAROUSEL

Violin

Lyrics by OSCAR HAMMERSTEIN II
Music by RICHARD RODGERS

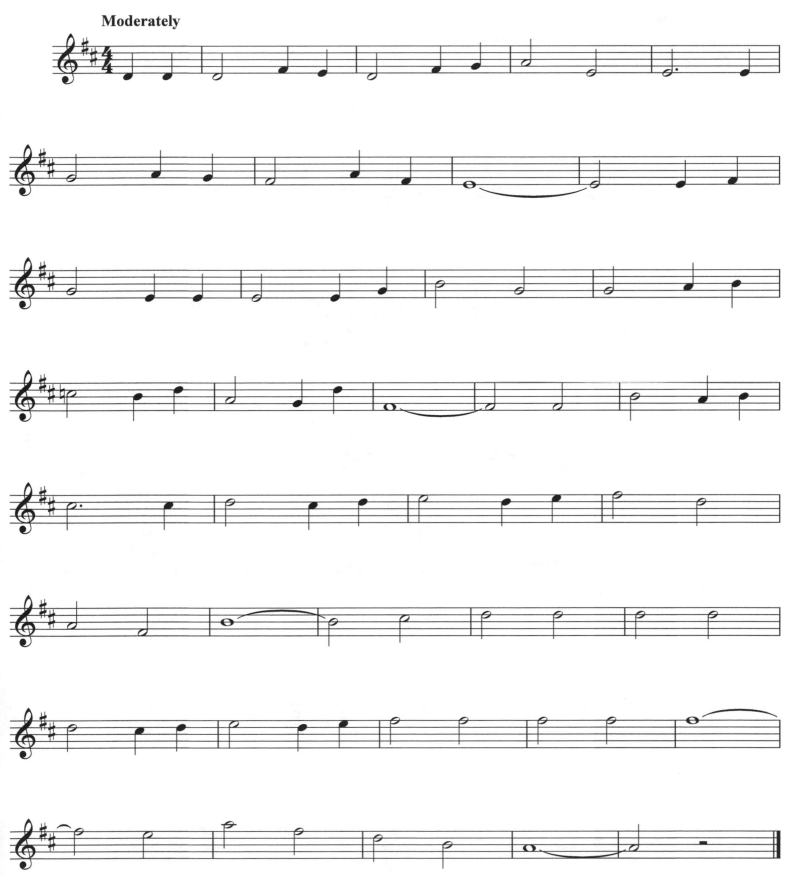

# YOU'LL BE IN MY HEART

Disney Presents TARZAN The Broadway Musical

VIOLIN

Words and Music by
PHIL COLLINS

**CODA**

# YOU'VE GOT A FRIEND

from BEAUTIFUL

VIOLIN

Words and Music by
CAROLE KING

# YOUNGER THAN SPRINGTIME

from SOUTH PACIFIC

VIOLIN

Lyrics by OSCAR HAMMERSTEIN II
Music by RICHARD RODGERS